BEHAVIOURAL INVESTING

UNDERSTANDING THE PSYCHOLOGY OF INVESTING

PAULINE YONG

For book orders, email orders@traffordpublishing.com.sg

Most Trafford Singapore titles are also available at major online book retailers.

Printed in Singapore.

ISBN: 978-1-4669-9896-4 (sc)
ISBN: 978-1-4669-9897-1 (e)

Trafford rev. 07/10/2013

 www.traffordpublishing.com.sg

Singapore
toll-free: 800 101 2656 (Singapore)
Fax: 800 101 2656 (Singapore)

DISCLAIMER

The material in this publication is of the nature of general comment only, and neither purports nor intents to be advice. Readers should not act on the basis of any matter in this publication without considering professional advice with due regard to their own particular circumstances. The author and publisher expressly disclaim all and any liability to any person, whether a purchaser of this publication or not, in respect of anything and of the consequences of anything done or omitted to be done by any such person in reliance, whether whole or partial, upon the whole or any part of the contents of this publication.

CONTENTS

PREFACE

While pursuing my MBA I came across the topic of Behavioural Finance and since then my perspective on the financial world has changed. Back in the early 1990's when I was a finance student in Canada I learned about the "Efficient Market Hypothesis" which said the market was always efficient and the price of a security always reflected the true value, any deviation was short term and was known as an anomaly (abnormal), it would be quickly adjusted by arbitragers that brought the price back to its true value. I was very puzzled because I found that what was taught in theory was very much different with what was going on in the real financial world.

Once I discovered Behavioural Finance I knew it should be an essential course for any finance student or practitioner. Behavioural Finance acknowledges the fact that human decisions are subject to several cognitive illusions and that human emotions often get in the way of successful investing. Hence, it becomes an essential course for any investor who wants to know more about the psychological aspects of investing. In fact, higher learning institutions not only offer Behavioural Finance to undergraduate students, but also to bankers and financial practitioners.

In this book, I will focus on Behavioural Finance as I believe this is an important lesson for all investors. When we buy a stock, we usually try to determine the fair value of a stock price by analyzing the fundamentals of the company; but we often neglect the fact that the other part of the puzzle is the behavior of the market participants that push prices away from their true value. We may end up buying a seemingly attractive stock which later ends up in losing money.

Let's ask ourselves did we buy stock at the time when everyone seems to make money in the stock market and we feel we should do the same? Did we buy simply because the stock has fallen to its year low and assume it will rebound in near term? These are common investors' mistakes that have been repeated over and over again. How do we avoid those mistakes as an investor? Does that mean we can't make money from the stock market?

Not to worry, statistics have shown that markets in the long run go through a series of upswings and downswings but progress in an upward manner. The stock market is full of opportunity to make money and accumulate wealth. The important thing is to acquire more investment knowledge, understand human weakness and try to minimize investment blunders so that we can trade profitably in the future.

SECTION ONE
INTRODUCTION

CHAPTER 1

What Is Behavioural Finance?

What Factors Determine Stock Price?

That's a multi-million dollar question!

You may think the answer is obvious. In fact, there are two schools of thought. The proponents of Efficient Market Hypothesis (EMH) think that the price of a stock is a reflection of its true value based on the information available on the company, the product and the market. Whereas the supporters of the Behavioural Finance believe that investor emotion pushes the price of a stock wildly above or below its fair value.

Andrew Lo, a finance professor at Massachusetts Institute of Technology (MIT) has cleverly integrated these two theories and developed the Adaptive Market Hypothesis. According to Lo, while the degree of market efficiency is related to environmental factors in the market, the magnitude of profit opportunities available and the adaptability of the market participants, the emotions of the market participants also play a big role in dictating stock prices.

1

The Adaptive Market Hypothesis follows Darwin's rules and explains why hedge funds proliferated during this decade. In the beginning of the twenty first century, conventional equity funds were suffering severe losses in the wake of the bursting of the internet bubble, but hedge funds managed to pose some decent gains. Hence, under Darwin's rule: "survival of the fittest", when hedge funds make profits, naturally money flows to that direction. They dominated trading volume and became the market movers.

What Is Behavioural Finance?

Behavioural Finance is the study of the influence of psychology on the behaviour of investors and their subsequent effect on markets. It combines the discipline of psychology and economics to explain why and how people make irrational or illogical decisions when they make investment decisions.

Although several definitions of Behavioural Finance exist, there is considerable agreement between them. Lintner[1] defines Behavioural Finance as being "the study of how humans interpret and act on information to make informed investment decisions". Olsen[2] asserts that "Behavioural Finance does not try to define rational behaviour or label decision making as biased or faulty; it seeks to understand and predict systematic financial market implications of psychological decision processes."

---

[1] Lintner, G. (1998). 'Behavioral finance: Why investors make bad decisions', *The Planner*, 13,1:7-8.
[2] Olsen, R. (1998). 'Behavioral finance and its implications for stock price volatility', *Financial Analysts Journal*, 54,2:10-18.

Are people rational?

Economists argue that people are rational. Rational people make decisions or judgement using reasoned thinking, based on facts, applying rules; and those decisions are consistent over time. How far is this true? Do you spend time in analysing mundane simple task such as what to eat, where to shop or what to wear? Very often we make these simple decisions based on intuition or "gut feeling". But when it comes to investment or children's education, we will spend more time to gather information, do some analysis and then make a decision. Hence, decision making is a complex process, involving both analysis and intuition: analysis involves computation and more "rational" thought, but is slower; intuition, by contrast, is much faster, less accurate, and relying on heuristics or "gut feeling".

A study conducted in United Kingdom shows that people with autism related disorders are less likely to make irrational decisions, and are less influenced by gut instincts. This is because of the tiny brain tissue called "amygdala" which is involved in processing human emotions. According to research, people with autism-related disorders have a different density of amygdale in their brains than others.

Further research done by a Nobel Prize winner, Professor Kahneman, the founder of behavioural finance found that this "amygdale" trigger the fear factor in our brain causing us to feel "risk", which can gets in the way of successful investing.

What is amygdale?

Deep in the center of your brain, level with the top of your two ears, lie two small, almond-shaped knobs of tissue called the amygdala (ah-mig-dah-lah). When you confront a potential risk, you will trigger this hot button of the brain that acts as an alarm system—shooting signals up to the reflective brain like warning flares. Because the amygdale is so attuned to big changes, a sudden crash of the stock market tends to be more upsetting than longer, slower decline, even if it is greater in total.

On October 19th, 1987, the U.S. stock market plunged 23%, so sparking the amygdala and disrupting the behaviour of millions of people for years. Anyone who has ever been a teenager knows that peer pressure can make you do things as part of a group that you might never do on your own. When the fear factor strikes, people tend to follow the herd; not because you want to but because it hurts not to. Neuroscientist Gregory Berns says, "social isolation activates some of the same areas in the brain that are triggered by physical pain". Hence, being part of a large group of investors can make you feel safer and less painful.

Neuroscientists discovered that amygdala is responsible for our fear, emotional responses, and social behaviour. As a result, during the event of a stock market crash, our bio-instinct will tell us to be part of the larger community by following the crowd's action.

In Professor Kahneman's research, he got together a group of people whose brains had been damaged due to tumour removal or accident, and let them play a little game with the other group of normal people. Starting with $20, each one flipped a coin and called it: heads or tails. If the participant called it correctly, he won $2.50. If he called it incorrectly, he would lose only $1. If he was feeling unlucky, he could pass.

Given the odds of winning were tilted to participants favour, any player who wanted to maximise his or her returns would never pass. But the result showed that the "normal" group passed more than the "damaged head" group. Does that mean the best investors are mental defective? No, the conclusion was that emotions get in the way of successful investing. Emotions cause participants to react to "illogical" ways by refusing to bet, even when the odds were clearly in their favour. The un-emotional players, by contrast, did the "rational" thing more often and won more money.

However, another study published recently claims the opposite view. It says "adding emotions to decision-making process can enhance creativity, engagement and decision efficiency". This is contrary to the popular belief that level headed people are more rational and make better decisions.

No matter whether we are cool headed or hot headed, rationality depends on how we see things and in whose perspective. If we apply our own reasoning to the event, we can come up with different results. I believe most people are rational in their own minds, even if we may think otherwise. Some investors would rather feel 'safe' than 'risky'. Others enjoy playing for short term gains even though it costs them more time and money. Some do not even realise they have made the wrong decision simply because they have made the wrong assumptions or are given the wrong information.

Did You Know?

A Neuroscience Perspective

Since behavioural finance is about how investors behave when making investment decisions, hence it is natural for researchers to take these brains into experiment. There are numerous breakthroughs that link investor's behaviour with brain function. For instance, a research done by Brian Knutson, a neuroscientist, was the study of how the brain works when making risky decision. A functional magnetic resonance imaging (fMRI) scan was used to capture images of a subject's brain while the subject is asked to perform certain task.

The experiment:

Nineteen subjects aged from 24 to 39, were given $20. In each round of the test, the volunteers got to choose among the following three investments and fMRI captures what was going on inside their brains as they made their trades:

- A bond that was guaranteed to return $1 per round.
- A safe stock, with 50 percent chance of earning $10 per round and a 25 percent chance of losing $10.
- A risky stock, with a 50 percent chance of losing $10 and a 25 percent chance of winning $10.

Before the students made a risky bet, their *nucleus accumbens* (a part of the brain) flashed yellow on Knutson's screen. This part of the brain is driven primarily by dopamine, a chemical that scientists believe produces pleasure and euphoria. When *nucleus accumbens* are triggered, investors generally think that they have high chances of winning.

Dopamine is hormone which affects brain processes that control movement, emotional response, and the ability to experience pleasure and pain. Be careful! It may cause addiction as studies have shown that cocaine and other drugs of abuse have similar effects of that of the dopamine.

When the participants made a safe investment, a different part of the brain, the *anterior insula*, was activated. While our *nucleus accumbens* may bring us to euphoria, our *anterior insula* is believed to hold us back with anxiety that can at times be irrational.

The *anterior insula* is primarily driven by two other neurotransmitters, serotonin and norepinephrine or also known as noradrenaline. While dopamine flows during our moments of pleasure, these two chemicals are secreted by the brain when we are fearful or anxious.

When we make trading decisions, our brains send two different signals: the first seeks profits; the second tries to avoid loss. According to Knutson's experiment, subjects who showed high activity in the *anterior insula* were 20 percent less likely to invest in risky stocks and such people might sell impulsively when markets turn against them.

CHAPTER 2

Stock Market Crashes and Manias

"Knowing others is intelligence; knowing yourself is true wisdom. Mastering others is strength; mastering yourself is true power." (Lau Tzu, founder of Taoism)

I happened to witness the euphoria of the Chinese stock market for myself when I was on a holiday coach tour in Beijin, China in 2006. During a rest stop I overheard our bus driver and tour guide talking together.

To my surprise, the driver, a middle aged well dressed man was studying the stock prices in a newspaper.

"What bad luck . . ." he groaned to the tour guide, Ms Zhang, a petite studious looking girl whose first job it was since graduating from university. "I bought P at RMB4 and sold for RMB4.50, now it's RMB5.50, I should have held the stock longer."

"Didn't I tell you not to sell, said Ms Zhang, "I'm still holding it! If I sell it now, I'll make RMB1.50 per share. No, I'm not going to sell, it's for long term, this is the buy-and-hold strategy that I learned from investment books."

Because I had been tracking the pulse of the stock markets including the Chinese stock market, I knew that the average price earning ratio for Chinese stocks was around 40 (later it went up to 50 at the peak in October 2007) at that time. So I asked: "Excuse me, sorry to interrupt, but I must congratulate both of you on making profits from the stock market. I'm interested in the stock market too. Can you share with me how to choose a stock (pretending I was a nerd)?"

Hearing my compliments Ms Zhang grinned and said, "Oh no, I'm learning too. Before I buy any stock, I usually check the stock's financial ratios from the newspaper. Like this P, when I first bought it, the PE was only 30, it was cheap compared to others. And they said the market will remain bullish since the Olympic Game is going to be held in China in 2008."

"Thank you for sharing that information with me, good luck with your investment!"

Full of optimism and hopes! Not at all worried about the price earning ratio reaching a bizarre level, and that worried me.

In 1929, Yale University economist Irving Fisher stated confidently: "The nation is marching along a permanently high plateau of prosperity." Five days later, the U.S. stock market crashed and America was ushered into the period of the Great Depression.

The Great Depression

The 1920's were a time of peace and prosperity in the U.S. It was after World War I, the economy was fuelled by increased industrialisation and of course, an enormous bull run in the stock market.

From 1921 to 1929, the Dow Jones rocketed from 60 to 400! Many investors became rich instantly. The success stories of these people had lured more people into the craze and soon stock market trading became American's favourite pastime. Investors mortgaged their homes or borrowed on margin to invest into the stock market. To the average investors, stocks were a sure thing and few people actually studied the fundamentals of the companies they invested in.

At the height of investors confidence and optimism disaster struck. In October, 1929 stock prices on the Dow Jones began to fall—and fall and fall. It was not only the stock prices. At the same time real estate values went into decline too.

Once the Dow began its fall, wide spread panic selling set in which led to the Great Depression that was to last for some six years in the American history.

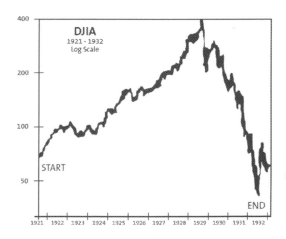

There were signs prior to the crash:

1. Rising Stock Prices

New investors entering the market, many who viewed it as easy way to get rich quick, helped inflate stock prices. From the above graph we can see the Dow Jones Index climbed steadily at an increasing rate from 1924 to 1929. Investors basically buy high sell higher, and even many economists believed that stocks were seen as safe during the euphoria period.

2. Relative easy monetary policy

At that time, banks made money readily available at lower interest rates to people to buy houses, cars and even stocks. Sounds familiar? Isn't this similar to the Alan Greenspan era of low interest rate policy in the early 2005 that led to the housing bubble and subsequently the subprime mortgage crisis in the U.S.?

3. Lack of stock market regulation

There was lack of effective legal guidelines on buying and selling stocks. Many investors in the stock market practiced "buying on margin", that is, buying stock on credit. Confident that the stock value would rise, an investor only paid a fraction of the total value of the stock, and sold the stock when the price went up. This would pay off the balance of their initial investment while reaping a hefty profit. This investment strategy turned the stock market into a speculative pyramid game, in which most of the money invested in the market did not actually exist.

4. Supply creates its own demand

Before the Great Depression, economists had strong belief in this macroeconomic theory that "supply creates its own demand". This theory holds that the production of goods and services created its own demand and that the economy would always be producing at full employment level. Hence, from 1925 on, industry was over-producing anticipating that whatever the production was, the goods would all be sold, which means, whatever the supply was, there would be demand for it. The increased production gave companies an aura of financial soundness, which encouraged Americans to buy more goods.

In summary, the history of financial manias and panics has been repeating over and over since the seventeenth century. From 1634 to 1636, "tulip mania" spread through Holland, causing the price of tulip bulbs to skyrocket to ridiculous levels, which wilted suddenly in 1636, creating widespread panic and financial dislocation. Other examples include England's South Sea Bubble of 1720, the U.S. Black Monday of 1987, the Japanese real estate bubble of the 1990's, the dot com era of 2000, the Asian financial crisis of 1997 and the 2008 financial crisis in the U.S. and the European countries.

There were a series of stages, beginning with a market or a sector that is successful, with strong fundamentals such as the banking sector. Then credit expands, and money flows more easily creating excess liquidity in the economy. For example, near the peak of Japan's bubble in 1990, Japan's bank were lending money for real estate purchases at more than the value of the property, expecting the value to rise quickly. As more money is available, prices rise. More investors are drawn in and expectations for quick profits rise. The bubble expands, and then finally burst.

There is only one phrase to describe the above phenomena—fear and greed. What we see over the past and today is that there were different themes of stock market crashes, but the same patterns occur over and over again. Humans are endowed with basically the same qualities (being fearful and greedy) today as they were in the seventeenth century.

Did You Know?

Tulip Bulb Mania

Back in 1593, a man by the name of Conrad Guestner imported the first tulip bulb into Holland from Turkey.

Few years later, tulip bulbs became a status symbol for the rich and famous. Initially, only the true connoisseurs bought tulip bulbs, but the rapidly rising price had attracted speculators looking for instant profits. It did not take long before the tulip bulbs were traded on local market exchanges, which were similar to today's futures market.

By 1636, tulip mania had feverishly spread to the Dutch middle class. Everybody was dealing in tulip bulbs futures contracts, looking to make a quick fortune. The majority of the tulip bulb buyers had no intentions of even planting these bulbs! The name of the game was to buy low and sell high, just like in any other market. The whole Dutch nation was caught in a sweeping mania!

Finally in February 1637, the tulip prices collapsed abruptly. Given that there were inconsistency of the price data, the extent of the tulip mania was difficult to estimate. Nevertheless Tulip Mania was one of the first market crash documented in history.

CHAPTER 3

The Limits to Learning

John Maynard Keynes, in his famous 1936 work, ``General Theory of Employment, Interest and Money,'' likened the stock market to beauty contests that ran in newspapers of his day, in which readers were asked to pick the prettiest face. The key to selecting the winner, Keynes argued, isn't choosing the face you think is the most beautiful but rather anticipating the face other people will pick.

Economic Nobel Prize winner, Kahneman started the Behavioural Finance theory with Tversky when they were conducting statistical research with a group of professional statisticians. They discovered that these experienced statisticians do not apply rules that they are aware of in computing the probability of statistical outcomes. They rely on their intuitions when it comes to simple problems given to them.

A typical, rational person chooses what options to pursue by assessing the probability of each possible outcome. For example, what is the likelihood of a given political party winning an election or the chances of surviving breast cancer? The answer is based on an assessment of the evidence collected through sampling and statistical calculation.

However, research conducted by Herbert Simon in 1955 proved that "full" rationality was an unrealistic standard for human judgment. Instead, he proposed a more realistic theory known as "Bounded Rationality" which acknowledged inherent processing limitations of the human mind. People reason and choose rationally, but only within the constraints imposed by their limited search and computational capabilities.

Building on Simon's work, Kahneman and Tversky introduced the idea of heuristics (mental shortcuts or intuitions). This idea means that people tend to use intuitions and biases to cope with their insufficient ability to process information fully rationally due to time pressure.

Heuristics are rules of thumb, educated guesses, intuitive judgment that help people to make decisions. These rules work well under most circumstances, but in certain cases may lead to cognitive bias.

Hence, when asked what is the survival rate for a stage 2 breast cancer patient? Like me, most of us are not medical practitioners and we tend to give a rough estimate based on our own experience. Person A whose relative recently died of breast cancer may probably give a lower rate than person B who has friends that survived the cancer pretty well. This is known as "availability heuristic" which will be discussed later in greater detail.

The correct answer is: according to American Cancer Society, the 5-year breast cancer survival rate for the stage 2 varies according to size of the tumour and whether or not cancer has spread to the lymph nodes.

If the breast cancer is less than 2 centimeters (cm) in diameter and has spread to lymph nodes under the arm, the survival rate is 88%-

92%. For larger tumour between 2-5 cm in diameters and has spread to the lymph nodes, the survival rate is 76%-81%.

However you may argue that all these numbers are subjected to errors too because there are many factors that affect the probability figures such as the age group, the races, the number of sample size, the participants lifestyle and eating habits and so on. You're right on!

Statistics help people to make good decisions about uncertain situations. They are based on a series of methods used to collect and analyse data for a given subject. Hence, there is no one right answer, simply because statistics done by different people will yield different results. The survival rate for breast cancer for a white female will only be considered statistically accurate if the research done by the American Cancer Society yields similar results with Canada and other cancer societies in the western countries.

Intuitively, a "rational" or "unbiased" answer will include the consensus of the majority of the population. What is perceived as "rational" in one person may be considered as "irrational" in another person, just like people from an African tribe wearing leather shoes is seen as "crazy", whereas it is perfectly normal to the rest of the world. A 90% survival rate for breast cancer in the developed countries is consider as normal but become unrealistic in developing countries. Hence, we must learn how to see things in different angles to make more rational and unbiased decisions.

Did You Know?

The South Sea Bubble

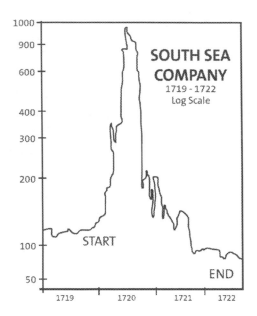

The mania started in 1711, after the war with France. The British government needed £10 million, so they proposed a deal to a financial institution, the South Sea Company by granting the exclusive trading rights to trade with the South Seas (now known as the South America). In return, South Sea Company would underwrite Britain's debt at 6% interest.

The South Sea Company began to issue stock to finance operations. Investors quickly saw what they perceived as value in the monopoly of the South America trade as everybody had heard of the gold and silver mines in Mexico and Peru.

It was believed that British manufactured goods were shipped to those places, the natives would pay for them with one hundred times their weight in gold and silver.

Shares were quickly snatched up. The South Sea Company, seeing the success of its first issue of shares, quickly issued even more. This stock was rapidly consumed by the voracious appetite of the investors.

By 1920, the whole nation was obsessed with trading the stocks of South Sea Company. Within short period of time, the price of South Sea Company ballooned ten times to £1,000 per share as shown in the diagram. Finally the bubble burst and the price crashed to almost nil.

SECTION TWO

TYPES OF
MENTAL BIASES

CHAPTER 4

Availability Bias

"Investors repeatedly jump ship on a good strategy just because it hasn't worked so well lately, and, almost invariably, abandon it at precisely the wrong time." David Dreman

If you were asked: "Which transportation is more risky: flying in an airplane or driving in a car? If we were logical we would judge the odds of risk by asking how often something bad has actually happened under similar circumstances. Instead, explains Kahneman, "We tend to judge the probability of an event by the ease in which we can call it to mind." The more recently it occurred, the more "available" an event will be in our minds—and the more probable its occurrence will seem.

Many people will think that the airplane is more risky as the tragedy of a plane crash is more vivid in our memory due to the wide extent of media coverage that sensationalise the whole incident.

However, statistics shown that more than 500 times as many people die on the U.S. roads as in airline accidents. There are other kinds of accidents that killed more people than aircraft crashes—stinging from bees and wasps, slipping on wet floors, choking on food, or falling down stairs!

However, you might say, "behind the wheel, we are in charge; in the passenger seat of a crowded aircraft, our lives lie in the hand of the pilots." Well, September 11 (or 911)'s tragedy did drive many previously confident flyers back on the roads. According to statistics, from October through December 2001, there were 1000 more highway fatalities than in the same period the year before partly because there were simply more cars on the roads.

Due to the availability bias, people pay attention to anything in the media that supports their fear and perception about flying; and ignore the other side of the story such as the information about the safety of flying. As a result, they abandon the safer transport (airplane) and opt for the riskier alternatives.

Many people have misconception about investing in the stock market too. When asked why they'd rather put their money in the bank than in the stock market, they say: "Why? Because I don't want to lose all my savings".

People typically give too much weight to recent experience and extrapolate recent trends that are at odds with long-run averages and statistical odds. They tend to become more optimistic when the market goes up and more pessimistic when the markets are down. These people probably heard one or two stories about people losing all of their savings in the stock market, but they ignore other facts about the stories—maybe those people invested on speculative stocks or they put all their eggs into one fragile basket. These people do not realise that by doing some research, they can find some safe and sound investments that produce greater returns than the bank rate.

Did You Know?

George Soros—The man who broke the Bank of England

Investors looking for a role model would find it hard to ignore George Soros, the billionaire hedge-fund manager. In 1992, he successfully pocketed one billion pounds by betting against the British pound and earning himself the name "the man who broke the Bank of England".

Unlike Warren Buffett, Soros is discrete about his investment strategy. He never gives detailed information about the holdings of his Quantum funds or his strategies. However, we can learn from his attitudes towards investment from his memoir book—"Soros on Soros".

In his autobiography, Soros said he does not hold to the common belief that markets are always right. However, this does not mean he simply bets against prevailing market trends since most of the time the market will continue to grow provided investors expect it to. "Everyone starts to believe stocks only go up, stocks will go up. Perception and reality go hand in hand."

A success factor for George Soros is that he is able to seek out the weaknesses inherent in an investment. In 1992, Soros had successfully identified the over-valuation of sterling and betted almost his entire Quantum fund in a short sell position on the pound. At that time, the Bank of England was the biggest loser as it was losing billions trying to artificially buoy up its currency.

Nevertheless, George Soros also made some wrong judgments too. In 1987, he failed to avoid the stock market crash and lost an estimated $800 million. In 1994, he guessed the outcome of U.S. and Japan trade talks wrongly, losing $600 million when the dollar fell against the yen.

Despite some setbacks, I must admit that George Soros is a great investor. First, he acts rationally and thinks independently. And secondly, he is an emotionally detached investor who can undertake enormous emotional disturbances when he is doing the opposite of everyone else.

CHAPTER 5

Representative Bias—
Do not judge the book by its cover!

"A decline in stocks is not a surprising event, it's a recurring event—as normal as frigid air in Minnesota . . . When your outdoor thermometer drops below zero, you don't think of this as the beginning of the next Ice Age. You put on your parka, throw salt on the walk, and remind yourself that by summertime, it will be warm outside."—Peter Lynch

Imagine you saw someone making an L-parking and that person did a bad job, would you think that the person behind the wheel is a male driver or a female driver? If your answer is the latter, then you are probably falling prey to representative heuristic.

We like to judge a book by its cover—we tend to stereotype the following persons: a petite lady with a soft voice must be a kindergarten teacher rather than a pilot; a fierce looking tanned guy looks more like a construction worker than a doctor; a plainly dressed teacher teaches better than a young, fashionable teacher.

The representative heuristic is the essence of how society is institutionally prejudiced. It is formed from childhood when as children, we were taught to learn by association—girls should wear skirts; boys should play with toy cars; all nurses are ladies; garbage men are uneducated and the list goes on. Hence, when making judgment we tend to ignore the statistical facts and are easily swayed by the representation of the incident.

Investors commit to this bias when they make judgements based on stereotypical decisions: "Citibank is one of the largest banks in the US, the government will not let it collapse!"

"Proton is our national car, it won't go bankrupt, and our government will bail them out."

We tend to make judgment of likelihood based on how well it matches our mental representation or stereotype. If the event is similar to our stereotype image, we are likely to believe that event; if the event is dissimilar to our mental representation, then we may have doubts in that event. There is no right or wrong answer for this.

When Citigroup suffered huge losses during the global financial crisis of 2008 and its stock price plunged from $45 to $0.99 within a year. Investors that opined with a representative bias in fact made huge profits from it! In the end, the United States government took a 36% equity stake in the company by converting US$25 billion in emergency aid into common shares with a US Treasury credit line of US$45 billion to prevent the bankruptcy of the largest bank in the world at that time.

In another example, investors who fall prey to representative bias did become victims in the investing world. In December 2008, amidst the financial crisis in U.S., Bernard Madoff, a well known fund manager was arrested for US$50 billion financial scam. Madoff told the FBI agents that: "It's all just one big lie, basically it was a giant Ponzi scheme!"

A Ponzi scheme is a fraudulent investment operation that pays abnormally high returns to investors who are paid from money put into the scheme by new investors, rather from real profit generated by share trading.

Many financial institutions, high net worth individuals and charitable organisations invested billions of dollars with this ex-chairman of Nasdaq.

"The fund generated consistent returns was part of the attraction", said one investor who was fooled by Madoff's well representation. Indeed, Madoff's fund generated average annual returns of around 8 percent since 2004.

Prior to this was the bankruptcy of the Lehman Brothers in September 2008. Many senior citizens in Hong Kong and Singapore invested in the Lehman Brother's "guaranteed mini-bonds". One of the retirees in his 60's who didn't want to be named, said: "I've invested all my hard earned savings of HK3 million in the mini bonds. I don't know what to do now as my heart is broken!" Before the collapse, Lehman Brother was the fourth largest investment bank in U.S. with high credit and investment ratings of triple A.

Here again, investors trusted that the bonds issued by this 158 year-old investment company were 100 percent secured. These innocent investors did not realise that in reality, not only were they exposed to the US housing market but also to a complex credit default swap arrangement!

Did You Know?

Even Warren Buffett was swayed by emotion

In the Berkshire Hathaway's 2009 letter to its shareholders, Warren Buffett admitted that he made at least one major investment mistake in the year of 2008.

The first mistake was investing a large amount in ConocPhillips stock when oil and gas prices were very near to the peak. Buffett said he did not anticipate the dramatic fall in energy prices in 2008, so this decision cost Bershire shareholders several billion dollars.

The second mistake was to buy $244 million on stocks in two Irish banks that appeared cheap. But since then, he has written down the value of those purchases to $27 million.

So what can we learn from "The Oracle of Omaha's" mistakes?

1. Be fearful when others are greedy.

Ironically this is the philosophy Buffett has been telling people. Indeed, the 2008 energy and commodities were a bubble that Buffett had warned people about, and yet he bought them.

2. Beware of the herd mentality.

Buffett's mistakes were testaments to the power of the herd instinct. We have to admit that there is so much havoc the market can play on investors' emotions that even Buffett was swept by the euphoria.

CHAPTER 6

Anchoring on Irrelevant Data

"The better we can understand how fear and greed are represented in individuals and how they react to market circumstances, the more likely we are to be able to avoid crises of these sorts,"—Andrew W. Lo, professor of finance at the Massachusetts Institute of Technology's Sloan School of Management

My uncle is a savvy investor who is the follower of Buy-and-Hold investment strategy. His portfolio consists of mostly blue chip stocks that he bought during the 1997 financial crisis. Over the past 12 years, his portfolio ballooned many folds and he did not sell them during the peak period.

One of the stock in his portfolio was IOI Corp. He saw the prices went from RM2 per share to RM8 per share and back to RM2 in 2008. When the stock was trading at RM3.50 I asked him: "Do you want to sell it?" He said no because he did not sell at RM8, why would he want to sell at RM3.50?

This is a common mental bias in our human nature that I'm going to talk about next.

Anchoring is a psychological bias that affects the way people intuitively assess value and probability. People use this heuristic when they start with an implicitly suggested reference point ("anchor") and then make adjustments to reach an estimated value.

An experiment was done to prove this theory. There were two groups of students given the following arithmetical expressions respectively and were to give an estimate within 5 seconds.

Group A: 1 x 2 x 3 x 4 x 5 x 6 x 7 x 8
Group B: 8 x 7 x 6 x 5 x 4 x 3 x 2 x 1

Group A made a median estimate of 512, while group B made a median estimate of 2,250. The motivating hypothesis was that students would try to multiply the first few factors of the product, then adjust upward. In both cases the adjustments were insufficient, relative to the true value of 40,320; but the group A's guesses were much more insufficient because they started from a lower anchor.

Similarly, investors always look at the historical price of a stock as the reference point and act on it. Proton used to be the darling of the stock market with prices around RM8-RM10 in the early 2000. However, due to Asean Free Trade Agreement (AFTA) and other competition, Proton's market share has plunged from 60% to 24% since 2000. When the stock price declined to RM6 in January 2006 many investors thought it was a bargain (as they reference from the high of RM10) and started to accumulate the stocks. Little did these investors know that Proton later fell to below RM2 two years later.

Investors like to predict stock prices based on their past performance. However, if you are the proponent of efficient market hypothesis where it says stock price follows "Random Walk" theory, there is no way you can predict the future price. Just like the fair coin game, the previous flips have no relation to the subsequent future flips.

I have many friends who practiced "buy low, sell high" strategy. They would only focus on a few blue chip stocks such as Maybank, Public Bank, and Genting, and buy them when their prices were near year low and try to sell them later at higher prices. So, what's the problem with this strategy?

The problem is that "buy low, sell high" is an axiom most investors understand but extremely difficult to implement. Let me tell you a story that happened during the Asian financial crisis in 1997. Mr. Ang was a faithful follower of Maybank, he has been trading in the stock market for many years and trading Maybank stock was his favourite as he had made profits on this stock many times. His strategy was to buy the stock when it went through the down cycle and sell it when it went up. As he made a few gains on the same stock he became confident and thought he could predict the trend. When the Asian financial crisis broke out, the price of Maybank fell to a level that he thought was the bottom so he invested heavily. Not only did he put all his savings on it, he even borrowed money to invest as he thought it was a sure gain. In the end, the stock did not recover but went further down and he was forced to cut loss.

The moral of the story: If we follow this rule blindly without doing some research on the stocks we are bound to lose money in the long term. Mr. Ang should be more cautious about banking stocks during financial crisis as banks are usually badly hurt by non-performing loans.

Financial decisions need to be based on relevant and correct facts in order to be considered valid. Anchoring is the tendency to attach thoughts to a reference point, even though there is no logical relevance for this. The next time when you see the price of any stock suddenly drops or increases by a lot, watch your own thinking. Are you adjusting a figure in search of an estimate? Try to think of an anchor in the opposite direction or come up with a new estimate entirely based on the latest information.

Did You Know?

Efficient Market Hypothesis (EMH)

For almost forty years, Efficient Market Hypothesis (EMH) has been the key proposition of traditional (neoclassical) finance. In Eugene Fama's classic paper—"Risk, Return, and Equilibrium", he defined EMH as the one in which security prices always fully reflect the available information.

For instance, on the event of a mining company discovers more iron ores, the share price of the mining company will jump up as soon as investors value the company based on its fundamental value, which is the present value of future cash flows, discounted by a rate appropriate to its risk level, then quickly bid up the share price of the mining company to reflect its true value immediately. Should there be any deviation from the fundamentals (caused by the minority irrational investors), the active and unlimited arbitragers will countervail and bring the prices back to right levels.

In theory, there are three forms of market efficiency:

1. Weak form—where stock prices reflect all past information in prices.
2. Semi-strong form—where stock prices reflect all past and current, public available information.
3. Strong form—where stock prices reflect all relevant information, including information that is not yet disclosed to the general public such as insider news.

Under the EMH, since market is efficient and stock prices follow Random Walk Theory, it is simply impossible to outperform the market consistently in the long run as prices are unpredictable and random.

Interestingly, this theory has attracted a lot of criticisms from many investment gurus such as George Soros, Peter Lynch and Warren Buffett due to the fact that these people are living examples of investors who can beat the market consistently over a longer investment horizon!

CHAPTER 7

Framing Effect: Half full or half empty?

"An investment said to have an 80% chance of success sounds far more attractive than one with 20% chance of failure. The mind can't easily recognise that they are the same".—Daniel Kahneman

Investors investing emotion can be greatly affected by the way business news are being interpreted. A typical negatively framed news coverage on the economy would be like this:

"Unemployment rate rose to an historical high in four years, further proving that the economic downturn is getting worse."

Here's how the same information can be framed positively:

"We are pleased to announce that the unemployment rate increased at a lower than expected rate. This shows that our economy has gone through the darkest moment and we are heading for a recovering."

Human cognitive decision can be strongly susceptible to the manner in which options are presented, this is known as the "framing effect". Research was done by psychologist, Dan Ariely where a group of people were given the same aspirin pills but under different labels— one as brand-name aspirin, the other as generic aspirin. The majority of the subjects believed that brand-name aspirin was more effective when the two pills were actually the same.

A rational decision maker should make an unbiased judgment no matter how the decision problem was framed. However, there exist some decision problems in which people systematically violate the rationality. For example, in the classic example from Kahneman and Tversky's 1981 article, participants are told that a new disease had surfaced that was expected to kill 600 people, and they must choose between pairs of unpleasant options aimed at combating the disease. The first set of choices is as follows:

Program A: 200 people will be saved with certainty.
Program B: 600 people saved with a probability of 0.33

Which would you choose?

When I present the above question to my economics students, most students choose program A. Although it's not a good plan but it guarantees 200 live. Next, I present a second set of options.

Program C: 400 people die for certain
Program D: 600 die with a probability of 0.67

Which would you choose?

Given these options, most students want to take a risk by adopting program D. With one-third chance of avoiding all deaths seem more appealing than the 400 certain deaths with program C. But the choices are exactly the same. The only difference between the first pair and the second is the way in which they are framed. Program A and B are presented in terms of the number of people "saved"; and program C and D described the number of deaths, but program A = program C, and program B = program D. So why do people prefer program A, the sure thing, in the first set of choices, but switch to program D, the risky option, in the second? Why are people more willing to take risks with negatively framed outcomes than with positively framed situations?

In order to answer that question, Kahneman and Tversky further proposed prospect theory which will be discussed in the next chapter.

CHAPTER 8

Loss Aversion: I hate losses!

Tversky makes the following speculation about this behaviour: "Probably the most significant and pervasive characteristic of the human pleasure machine is that people are much more sensitive to negative than to positive stimuli . . . [T]hink about how well you feel today, and then try to imagine how much better you could feel . . . [T]here are a few things that would make you feel better, but the number of things that would make you feel worse is unbounded."

Here's the Theory

Extending on the framing effect, "loss aversion" also known as "prospect" theory describes how an individual behaves when face with a risky situation. This theory suggests that when we are presented with choices, we consider the effects of each option relative to our present

35

circumstances. Will we gain or lose relative to our current status quo? Definitely, we prefer gains. It is always better to receive money than to lose it. It is always better to save lives than to lose them. But Kahneman and Tversky's crucial contribution was the recognition that losses and gains are not weighed equally—for the same amount of gains and losses, losses hurt more than gains. The following is an experiment conducted involving two separate groups of experimental subjects to prove the theory.

Group A and B were presented the following two questions:

Question A:

In addition to whatever you own, you have been given $1000. You are now asked to decide whether to accept a sure $500 gain or take a gamble. The gamble features a 50-50 chance of winning $1000 more or nothing more.

Question B:

In addition to whatever you own, you have been given $2000. You are now asked to decide whether to accept a sure $500 loss or take a gamble. The gamble features a 50-50 chance of losing $1000 or nothing.

The options given to both groups have the same average result of $1500. If the experimental subjects behaved logically they should had no particular preference for either of the choices that they were presented with. The results of the experiment were not as expected. 84% of group A opted for the sure gain and 15% went for the chance; on the other hand, 31% of group B took the sure loss and 69% the chance.

Like the disease problem, the results indicated that when people are presented with gains they tend to choose the sure and guaranteed option. On the other hand, when they are presented with losses they tend to take more risk. Hence, when faced with sure gain, most investors are risk-averse, but faced with sure loss, investors become risk-takers. In addition, individuals are much more distressed by prospective losses than they are happy by equivalent gains. Some economists have concluded that investors typically consider the loss of one dollar twice as painful as the pleasure received from a one dollar gain.

Now back to the disease problem, the 400 deaths carries substantial negative weights. If there is a chance to avoid this big hurt, people are more likely to take on more risk by choosing program D instead of program C.

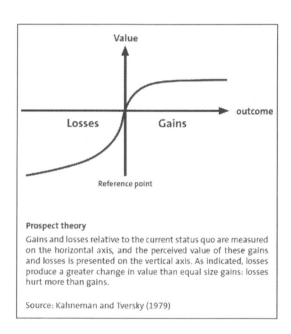

Prospect theory

Gains and losses relative to the current status quo are measured on the horizontal axis, and the perceived value of these gains and losses is presented on the vertical axis. As indicated, losses produce a greater change in value than equal size gains: losses hurt more than gains.

Source: Kahneman and Tversky (1979)

There are other examples in our daily lives that show people tend to be more sensitive to negative than to positive stimuli. For instance in school, when students are told that for each true and false question, each correct answer will be awarded one mark and for any wrong answer one mark will be deducted; students will spend more time to prepare for the test because the lost of marks is very painful to them.

Sell the Winners, Hold on to the Losers

Similarly, investors feel more comfortable taking a profit on an investment than selling an under-performing stock at a loss. Investors are more likely to take comfort from paper loss than establishing a real loss.

For instance, if you need to sell stocks in your portfolio to raise money, you have two stocks: stock A, a promising stock, is currently making a 20% profit; stock B, an average stock, is making a loss of 20%, which stock will you sell? Most investors would choose to sell stock A.

Many investors will not sell anything at loss. This common investor behaviour is due to the theory of loss aversion. They don't want to give up the hope of making profits for a particular investment. Even if they need the money urgently, they would rather sell those winners first.

They have high hopes that the price of the stock will recover and often focus on returning to a neutral position before exiting. This 'get even' attitude has probably wrought more destruction on investment portfolios than bear markets.

Hence, the understanding of prospect theory is extremely useful for an investment manager in obtaining a clearer understanding of shareholders' perceptions towards investment. It acknowledges that investors focus on gains and losses of individual investments and not on the overall picture. Emphasis is also given more to losses than to gains, to the extent that losses are more painful after prior losses and subsequently lead to a greater risk of further irrational decisions.

CHAPTER 9

Mental Accounting—
Splurging on windfall money

"Psychology is probably the most important factor in the market—and one that is least understood."—Dreman David

Suppose you are going to a movie and as you enter the cinema, you discover that you have lost your movie ticket you've just paid $10 for. Would you spend another $10 to get a new one? If you are like most people, you would probably think twice because you will feel that you will end up paying $20 for a movie actually worth $10!

Now let's construct the scenario differently. You are going to see a movie. On your way to the movie theatre you drop a $10 note on the bus. You are disappointed, of course, but would this affect your decision to buy the movie ticket? You will probably say to yourself:

"Damn it! That's my luck!" Arriving at the cinema, you will forget about the incident and stand in line to get a movie ticket.

In fact, the above research was conducted by some psychologists who discovered that only 46 percent of those who lost a ticket were willing to buy a replacement ticket, whereas 88 percent of those who lost an equivalent amount of cash were willing to buy a ticket. Since the lost ticket and the lost cash had the same value, their loss should have been experienced in the same way, but why were there twice as many people willing to ignore the lost cash but not the lost ticket? Why is it that you feel more pain in losing the movie ticket than the ten-dollar note?

This is due to a psychological phenomenon proposed by the famous psychologist, Richard Thaler, known as mental accounting. It says that people tend to separate and categorise income and expenses into different accounts in their heads. For example, you might have an entertainment fund, an investment fund, an education fund for children and so on.

Losing a movie ticket and having to buy a second one takes $20 out of your entertainment fund when you planned to take only $10, so it's "out of my budget"!

Many of us commit this mental mistake in our daily lives without realising it. For example, we treat the company bonuses, capital gains from selling stocks, dividends and tax refunds as a "windfall" source other than our normal source of income. We splurge on luxury items such as LV bags, Caribbean Cruise and Rolex watches with this "windfall" money in spite of having a housing loan and a car loan due for payments.

Somehow we have grouped our income and expenditure into separate mental "funds" or "budgets" that are not easily combined. Money received as part of our salary is treated differently from money received as a bonus. Similarly, money spent to buy a fixed asset is viewed differently from the same amount of money spent to treat ourselves to a dinner at a luxury restaurant.

From an economic perspective, these mental accounting rules violate the economic principle of "fungibility", which means that all money is equal. A dollar is still a dollar whether you get it as a gift from a friend or from your salary. Hence, when the principle of fungibility is violated, people act in economically irrational ways.

If you receive a pay raise of $500 per month, you are less likely to go on a spending spree compared to a situation where you receive a bonus of $500. We will treat the pay raise as the regular source of income; and treat the $500 bonus as "windfall" income, even though your income has increased by the same amount at the end of the month.

Mental accounting is not without its benefits. If you put aside some money for retirement you will try to protect this account in your mind by not spending it. But when it comes to investing in unit trusts investors like to arbitrarily divide the components of total returns into capital appreciation and income return such as dividends.

Unit trust holders are often fooled by the fact that when their funds declare dividends, the dividends are actually paid out from the fund's net assets. Unlike stocks dividend, the unit trust dividends are not extra gains but more like enjoyment of your unit's progress with suitable reduction of the fund's net asset value after dividend payment.

Stock investors often apply mental accounting when making investment decisions. We have the tendency to treat capital gains as windfall money and indulge in luxury goods with the profits. Imagine how much money we can accumulate if we simply reinvest the money into various forms of investment and let our money grow for us.

So the next time you are thinking of splurging your year-end bonus or capital gains on an exotic vacation, think about the fungibility of money. There are no labels attached to the money you receive or spend. The labels you attach to your income and expenditure are all in your mind!

Did You Know?

Capital Asset Pricing Model (CAPM)

The Capital Asset Pricing Model (CAPM) was developed by William Sharpe in 1970. This is a brilliant pricing model for securities, which means if you know the beta (see the next Did You Know) of a stock, you can generate the stock's return using the CAPM formula.

CAPM Formula:

$$\bar{r}_a = r_f + \beta_a \left(\bar{r}_m - r_f \right)$$

Where :
r_f = Risk free rate
β_a = Beta of the security
$\bar{r}_m$ = Expected market return
$(\bar{r}_m - r_f)$ = Equity market premium

The risk free rate is 5% as we take the return of a bond and the expected market return of around 8%, hence the only unknown is the beta which is company specific. Once we know the beta of a specific company we may generate the expected return of that particular stock.

In theory, if you do not want any risk, invest in government bond and be happy with your 5% return. However, if you demand higher return you must be able to tolerate higher risk (beta) since the formula states that the higher the beta (or inherent risk) of the company, the higher the expected return. This explains why your financial advisor always tells you—high risk high return!

CHAPTER 10

Gambling Behaviour and Speculation

"Speculation is an effort, probably unsuccessful, to turn a little money into a lot. Investment is an effort, which should be successful, to prevent a lot of money from becoming a little."—Fred Schwed Jr.

Gambling Behaviour

Many researchers believe that it is human nature to gamble and take unnecessary risks.

One aspect of gambling behaviour is known as the "gambler's fallacy" which is related to the representative heuristic. People who fall prey to gambler's fallacy fail to understand statistical independence and he or she would make a statement like this: "I've lost three nights in a row. I will win big tonight". These people believe that the outcome of the result can be controlled by luck, skills or specific events. This is

43

incorrect reasoning because each event is independent of the other as past events will not change the probability of the future ones.

For example, consider that 50 cent coin flips have all landed with the "heads" side up 6 times in a row. What is the probability of the next coin flip being a "tail"? If you think that the chances of flipping a "tail" are very high, more than 50%, then you have committed the Gambler's Fallacy. The coin flipping is a fair game which means the likelihood of a fair coin turning up heads is always 50%. Each coin flip is an independent event, which means that any previous flips will not affect the result of the future flips.

Many investors believe that they should sell stock that has gone up for several consecutive days, as it's highly unlikely that it will go up further. Similarly, investors might hold on to a stock that has fallen in multiple sessions because they view further decline is improbable.

Speculation

According to Benjamin Graham, the teacher of Warren Buffett, if an operation does not follow the principles of "safety of return" and "adequacy of return", then it is classified as speculation not investment.

The great economist, John Maynard Keynes once said, "Speculation is the activity of forecasting the psychology of the market."

Speculators are everywhere. They can speculate on anything—be it property, oil price, currency, commodity, warrant or stock, as long as there is opportunity for making quick profits. If someone thinks that property prices are going to rise but he already owns a house, then he is a speculator if he buys a property now and attempt to sell it later at higher price.

Hence, a speculator makes predictions of future price movements based on the available market information and the psychology of the market.

George Soros understands the concept thoroughly and warned people about the risk as a speculator: "It's not whether you're right or wrong that's important, but how much money you make when you're right and how much money you lose when you're wrong."

I would rather be a rational investor than a speculator as I know that any investment decision based on hearsay or guessing is usually unpredictable, short-term and unwarranted.

Did You Know?

What is Beta?

Beta is a measure of a stock's volatility in relation to the market. In this case, the market refers to Dow Jones Industrial Average (DJIA). By definition, the market has a beta of 1.0 and individual stocks are ranked according to how much they deviate from the market.

A stock that moves exactly with DJIA has a beta exactly equals to 1.0. If a stock swings more than the DJIA given a fixed period of time, the beta will be more than 1.0 which means the stock is quite volatile and it happens to be more risky. Similarly, if a stock swings less than the market, the beta will be less than 1.0 and it means the stock is less volatile than DJIA.

The calculation for beta coefficient is based on the correlation of volatilities between a stock and the DJIA. In other words, the relative risk of a security is compared to the risk of the DJIA through regression analysis.

For example, after a series of calculation, we obtain a beta coefficient of 2. This means that if the market goes up by 3%, the stock will move up by 6%. Similarly, if a stock has a beta coefficient of -2, this means when the market is advanced by 3%, the stock will decline by 6%.

Beta Coefficient	Related Stock Price Change
ß > 1	The related stock is cyclical and volatile. For example: growth stocks, hi-tech stocks.
ß = 1	The stock moves in tandem with the market or KLCI.
ß < 1	The stock is less volatile compared with the market. For example: defensive stocks.
ß =0	The stock's return is independent of the market. For example: the Merdeka bond.
ß = Negative	The stock is moving in the opposite direction of the market.

The main advantage of knowing the beta of a stock is when you need to construct a portfolio. You need to assess the inherent risk of individual stocks to meet the diversification objective. In theory, if you have a stock with +1.0 beta and another stock with -1.0 beta, you have actually bring down the overall risk of your portfolio to nil. However, a major drawback is the fact that beta coefficient is based on historical data which does not tell us much about the future. A company may have a low beta coefficient now may turn out to have much higher beta in the future if there is a change in its management.

CHAPTER 11

Overconfidence

"There are two main implications of investor overconfidence. The first is that investors take bad bets because they fail to realize that they are at an informational disadvantage. The second is that they trade more frequently than is prudent, which leads to excessive trading volume."—Hersh Shefrin, author of Beyond Greed and Fear

Overconfidence

One of the most documented of all psychological errors is the tendency to be over optimistic. In general, most people do not see the need to improve the way they make decisions, as they believe that they are already making excellent decisions. The unwarranted belief that we are usually correct is a major real-life barrier to critical thinking.

People exaggerate their own abilities and this is particularly common in managing their assets. Overconfidence often results in investors being fooled by small gains in a few trades, feeling much more in control of a situation than they are. Money managers, advisors and investors are consistently overconfident in their ability to outperform the market, but fail to do so.

For example, mutual fund managers, analysts, and business executives at a conference were asked to write down (1) how much money they would have at retirement and (2) what is their net worth now. The average figures were $5 million and $2.6 million respectively. The professor who asked the question said, "regardless of the audience, the ratio is always 2:1". People are definitely very confident that they will at least make more money in future than now.

Overconfidence can lead to the followings:

Not having an investment plan

Perhaps the most common reason why investment plans fail is that the investor doesn't actually have a plan. The very first step of a rational investor is to draft a plan stating investment goals and conditions. This is to make you detached from the whole investment business and follow strictly by the book not your heart.

Overtrading

In Odean and Barbet's study of 78,000 investors' accounts in a large brokerage firm from 1991-1996, the most active traders scored an average return of 10% compared to the less active investors' 17.5% profits. And online traders suffer even lower returns as they tend to overtrade and thus lose money to brokerage charges.

Lack of diversification

Due to overconfidence, investors tend to invest heavily on a particular investment with the optimism that it will generate good returns. This lead to insufficient diversification of portfolios.

In general, overconfidence is caused by mental bias that leads investors to over-estimate their knowledge, under estimate the risk and exaggerate the control they have over a situation.

Did You Know?

Overconfidence

1. 19% of people think they belong to the richest 1% of U.S. households.
2. 82% of people say they are in the top 30% of safe drivers.
3. 80% of students think they will finish in the top half of their class.
4. 68% of lawyers in civil cases believe that their side will prevail
5. 81% of new business owners think their business has at least a 70% chance of success.
6. 86% of Harvard Business School classmates say they are better looking than their classmates.
7. When asked to make a prediction at the 98% confidence level, people are right only 60-70% of the time.
8. Graduate students were asked to estimate the time it would take them to finish their thesis under three scenarios: best case, expected, and worst case. The average guesses were 27.4 days, 33.9 days and 48.6 days, respectively. The actual average turned out to be 55.5 days.

(Source: T2 Partners LLC)

CHAPTER 12

Herd Mentality

"Although markets do tend toward rational positions in the long run, the market can stay irrational longer than you can stay solvent."—John Maynard

First we must acknowledge that the phenomenon of the herd mentality can be useful in many ways. For example, research shows that although 5% of the animals in a herd know the location of the water source, the entire herd is able to find it. In our daily lives, we use this instinct to navigate to the exit in cinemas and crowded streets.

We have to admit that herding is our human instinct. Herding always makes us feel comfortable, and being the odd one out make us feel uneasy. We are programmed to feel that the consensus view must be correct one; and this mistaken belief has led to many disastrous decisions such as the "Four Dragons" and "Four Tigers Era" of the 1990's where many investors who were initially sceptical ended up buying into the hype under the mistaken belief that not everyone could be wrong. And yet, most people were wrong.

Some researchers theorise that investors follow the crowd and conventional wisdom to avoid the possibility of feeling regret in the event that their decisions prove to be incorrect.

Fear of Regret

People tend to feel sorrow and grief after having made an error of judgment. Investors deciding whether to sell a security are typically emotionally affected by whether the security was bought for more or less than the current price.

For example, most investors avoid selling stocks that are making paper losses in order to avoid the pain and regret of having a bad investment. The mentality is: after all, it's only a paper loss, as long as I don't realise the loss, it doesn't count!

In addition, investors have the mindset of "what if the price goes up after I've sold it"; hence they would rather hold on to bad stocks hoping one day it will turn into a star.

However, some professional traders even advocate trend following as their winning trading strategy. They would apply technical analysis to help them in identifying the prevailing trend and trade with the trend. The biggest pitfall of this method is that it ignores fundamental analysis totally.

Herd mentality can be for good or bad. It is not totally wrong to follow the herd, but we must know when to follow and when not to. The challenge is in making an educated guess about when a turning point will occur and developing a trading plan to capitalise on it.

Did You Know?

Conforming with the crowd: Solomon Asch experiment

In 1950's, a Social psychologist Solomon Asch conducted an experiment to test whether perfectly normal human beings can be pressured into unusual behaviour by authority figures, or by the consensus of opinion around them.

In his experiment, eight subjects were seated around a table, only one participant was actually a genuine subject for the experiment, the rest were experiment associates, carefully trained to give certain pre-selected responses.

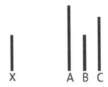

Each participant was asked to answer a series of questions such as which line was the longest, which line matched the reference line, etc (Figure 1). The participants provided a variety of answers, at first correct, to avoid arousing suspicion in the subject, but then some incorrect responses added later on.

In a control group, with no pressure to conform to a different view, only one subject out of 35 gave an incorrect answer. However, the result for the other group was interesting indeed. When surrounded by people giving incorrect answer, over one third of the subjects also voiced an incorrect opinion. At least 75% of the subjects gave the wrong answer to at least one question, although experimental error may have had some influence on this figure. There was no doubt that peer pressure can cause conformity.

(Source: Solomon E. Asch, "Studies of independence and conformity: A minority of one against a unanimous majority", Psychological Monographs, 70)

CHAPTER 13

Confirmation Bias and Cognition Dissonance

"The greatest challenge for value investors is maintaining the required discipline. Being a value investor usually means standing apart from the crowd, challenging conventional wisdom, and opposing the prevailing investment winds. It can be a lonely undertaking. A value investor may experience poor, even horrendous, performance compared with that of other investors or the market as a whole during prolonged periods of market overvaluation."—Seth Klarman

Confirmation Bias

Confirmation bias is a behavioural flaw of human beings by which once we have made a decision, we tend to actively seek information that will confirm our decision. Without realising it, we emphasise information which reinforces our view whilst tending to downplay, avoid or even ignore contradictory information.

A clear indication of this was the Chinese stock market bubble in 2007. Many market participants claimed there were clear signs of overvaluation in the Chinese A shares and B shares with average price earning ratio as high as 50. Obviously, stock prices were pushed up by speculators who were optimistic about the China's buoyant economy and the hosting of the Olympic Games. As a result, Chinese investors were buying into the euphoria.

Cognitive Dissonance

Cognitive dissonance is similar to confirmation bias. It states that when we hold two conflicting beliefs in our minds, the discomfort caused by this conflict drives us to acquire, or modify current beliefs in an attempt to relieve the conflict we feel.

Suppose you are told by your best friend that you should buy Maybank instead of Public Bank, as he tells you that he has insider's information that Maybank is going to declare better than expected earnings. However, after you've bought Maybank, you come across some analyst reports that Public Bank is better than Maybank. Thus, you have conflicting cognitions in your mind, which causes you the discomfort (dissonance), and to alleviate this discomfort, you tend to filter out this new information and seek out support for your preference belief.

Cognitive dissonance initiates a form of self-deception. How often do we see this scenario played out in the movies? The leading lady falls in love only to find later that her lover is a married man. How does she handle this distressing news? Often by distorting or ignoring the unpalatable facts. Just like real life.

Hence, it is important for an investor to constantly re-evaluate positions and views and change them as the situation requires and new data becomes available. It is inevitable that investors are going to make mistakes when forecasting the future. The good investors will minimise the financial damage done by such errors and the poor investors will fail to minimise the damage and this can lead to small number of errors causing large losses.

Did You Know?

The Contrarian Investment Guru—David Dreman

According to Dreman, investors cannot follow through simple strategies to beat the market because they are prone to overreaction and underreaction. His strategy is: Buy low price-earning ratio (PE) and out-of-favour stocks.

Since surprises are common in the financial markets, if you own favourites or glamour stocks, you'll get clobbered by negative surprises but will not get much upside movement by positive news; whereas if you own low PE and out-of-favour stocks, you will hardly be penalised for negative surprises but will be rewarded handsomely by positive surprises.

This sounds very logic even though Dreman found that even people who had an idea of this concept often did not follow it. Part of the reason is due to the overly optimistic nature in human. People have unrealistic optimism about future events, thinking such events will come out as what they predicted and they are in control of the situations. Yet in reality, both positive and negative surprises are bombarding the financial world every day.

Due to human's fear and greed nature, investors are generally overreacted to over-valued glamour stocks. Investors will push the favourite stocks overly high in the event of positive surprises; and send the stock tumbling in the event of negative surprises.

Out-of-favour stocks are better because these stocks are already under-valued in the first place, they will not fall much in the event of negative surprises, however, should there be any positive surprises, and these stocks will soar due to the overreaction of investors!

CHAPTER 14

Fear And Greed

"Graham's conviction rested on certain assumptions. First, he believed that the market frequently mispriced stocks. This mispricing was most often caused by human emotions of fear and greed. At the height of optimism, greed moved stocks beyond their intrinsic value, creating an overpriced market. At other times, fear moved prices below intrinsic value, creating an undervalued market."—Robert G. Hagstrom, The Warren Buffett Way

Fear and greed are the two emotions that rule the stock market. In the past we have seen many stock market crashes such as the tulip mania, the South Sea bubble, the Great Depression, the Asian financial crisis and so on. Investors do not seem to learn from these financial lessons.

In the case of Madoff, seasoned investors were apparently sucked into the alleged fraud despite their better judgment because they found his returns too tempting to pass up. In the case of the Lehman's mini-bonds, investors were lured by the promised yield without investigating the underlying risk as it was a relatively new product in the market. In the case of subprime martgages, homeowners who knew they could not afford certain homes proceeded nonetheless, because of the possible housing price appreciation was too attractive to pass up.

So when losses started to accumulate, investors' fear kicked in and panic ensued. A flight-to-safety in human instinct will lead to a stock market crash eventually.

This is the stock market cycle that every investor should be aware of. By understanding the cycle and human weakness, we can take advantage of the down cycle by accumulating under-valued blue chip stocks.

A U.K. survey in March 2009 showed that a third of British adults see the stock market as "good investment opportunities". At the time of survey, the FTSE 100 index (British stock market) recorded at 3800 down 40% from 6700 a year ago. However, when asked whether they have started investing in the stock market, only three percent said they were planning to take the plunge.

Why? The biggest fear is the fear of unknown. We never know how low the stock prices could go so better stay away. And when the stock market recovers, we are doubtful, we fear that it may not be sustained, we end up missing the opportunity.

As Warren Buffet says:

"We simply attempt to be fearful when others are greedy and to be greedy only when others are fearful."

We know the idiom perfectly well, but how many of us can actually overcome our fear factor and take the plunge? That's because of amygdale working in our brain that makes us feel the risk that suggests a high degree of risk aversion.

Did You Know?

Volatility Index (VIX)

In 1993, a new measurement for the index of volatility for the S&P 500 stock index came out with the purpose of measuring fear and greed. It is called the "VIX". If the VIX index goes up, the traders and investors may be heading for the exits. Conversely, if the VIX goes down, confidence and optimism are restored, money is coming off the sidelines and moving into equities.

We cannot trade the VIX directly but the VIX is traded on the futures exchange and can be traded just like any other investments. In general, VIX values greater than 30 are generally associated with a large amount of volatility as investors are fearful of uncertainty; VIX values less than 20 associate with less volatility and less stressful in the market.

On the other hand, when the VIX is consistently below 20, it means that the underlying S&P is in overbought position and it is due for a correction and vice versa.

There are 4 variations of the volatility index: the VIX tracks the S&P 500, the VXN tracks the Nasdaq, the VXD tracks the Dow Jones Industrial Average and the RVX tracks the Russell 2000. Investors can trade VIX futures for hedging purpose. For example, if VIX starts to rise, it means the level of fear and uncertainty is increasing and you may purchase VIX futures contracts on the Chicago Board Options Exchange (CBOE). If the market does indeed start to sell off and the VIX rises, the profits gained by the VIX futures can help to offset some of the losses that you might experience in other investments.

(Source: Investopedia)

SECTION THREE
PRACTICAL ADVICE FOR INVESTORS

CHAPTER 15

Can Heuristics Make Money

"Heuristics are rules of thumb, educated guesses, intuitive judgment that help people to make decisions. These rules work well under most circumstances, but in certain cases may lead to cognitive bias." Daniel Kahneman

The Positive Side of Heuristic and Bias

Heuristic is important in our daily lives as it often leads to quick solutions. Consider how players catch a ball—in baseball, badminton, or soccer. It may seem that they would have to solve complex differential equations in their heads to predict the trajectory of the ball. In fact, players use a simple heuristic. Whether a ball comes in high or low, the player will respond accordingly based on his or her past experience.

In Gerd Gigerenzer's book, "Simple Heuristics That Make Us Smart", the current world of limited knowledge and pressing time, simple heuristics enable smart choices to be made quickly and with a minimum of information by exploiting the way that information is structured in particular environments.

Gigerenzer gave the example of a man being rushed to hospital with an emergency heart attack. The doctor needed to decide whether the victim should be treated as a low risk or a high risk patient and that decision can save or cost a life! Based on available cues and past results of each of the many measurements that are taken when a heart attack patient is admitted, the doctor will make intelligent decisions and treat the victim accordingly.

Despite limiting search and processing, simple heuristics perform comparably to more complex algorithms, particularly when generalising to new data. Here is another simple story. In a study conducted by Gigerenzer and Goldstein in which they asked two groups of people, the Americans and the Germans which city have more inhabitants—San Diego or San Antonio? About two-thirds of the American participants answered correctly which is: San Diego. The German participants, who know much less about the American cities were hundred percent correct! The German participants had not heard of San Antonio, so they picked San Diego.

This is an interesting case of a smart heuristic, where people with less knowledge can do better than people with more. Heuristic works because in the real world there is a correlation between name recognition and its population. In fact, in many situations people like to choose products or services with name recognition, be it consumer household products or financial investment products. This is because consumer behaviour perceives brand names as quality and assurance.

Can Heuristics Make Money?

A study was conducted in the U.S. involving two groups of people, both pedestrians and business students. The researchers went to downtown Chicago and interviewed several hundred pedestrians.

They were given a list of stocks and were asked one question: Have you ever heard of this stock? Yes or no? The answers were recorded. Next, the researchers took the 10% of the stocks that had the highest recognition, which were all in the Standard & Poor's Index, put them in a portfolio and let them go for half a year. As a comparison, the researchers asked the business students to recommend stocks that are of lower recognition but fundamentally sound, put them in a portfolio and ran them for the same period as the other portfolio. After six months, the portfolio containing the highest recognised stocks by ordinary people outperformed the low recognition stocks in six out of eight cases.

Here again, this experiment has demonstrated that by applying simple heuristic rules, ordinary people can actually beat people that have more knowledge.

However, experiments are random and the results can be heavily influenced by external factors. If the above experiment was conducted during a bull run, of course the highest recognition stocks perform better.

The point is heuristics are important in our lives but can lead to serious mistakes if we take heuristics for granted without further investigating. For example, doctors often apply heuristics in their decision making as they have to make rapid decisions, either because of medical emergency or because they need to see many patients in a limited time. As a result, misdiagnoses inevitably occur. Recent medical research revealed that young adults with stroke symptoms are sometimes misdiagnosed in emergency rooms, causing the young stroke patients to miss the first hours of critical treatment. Because the chance of strokes in this age group is low doctors sometimes misdiagnose patients.

When investors apply heuristics, it may work occasionally but it will never work in the long term. Sometimes one bad judgement is enough to cost an investor his or her lifesavings.

CHAPTER 16

How to Overcome Your Emotion

"Successful investors tend to be unemotional, allowing the greed of others to play into their hands. By having confidence in their own analysis and judgment, they respond to market forces not with blind emotion but with calculated reason." Seth Klarman

In the present scenario, behavioural finance is becoming an integral part of the decision-making process, because it heavily influences investors' performance. It can improve investors' performance by recognising the biases and errors of judgement to which all of us are prone. Understanding behavioural finance will help investors to select a better investment and avoid repeating expensive errors in future. This chapter describes how we can minimise or eliminate psychological bias in the investment process.

Investment Plan

It is always advisable to write an investment plan before you trade. The virtue of the investment plan is to help you to stick to your original strategy without being influenced by the "noise" of trading.

In the plan, you need to write down policies and procedures of your investment in advance so that you don't jump from decision to decision. Try not to make your choice based on what the stock market is telling you or what other people are doing. Make your investment decision based on a proper investment plan that has been working for you consistently and which you feel comfortable with.

Diversify Your Portfolio

A portfolio invested primarily in one market sector is too risky as investors may end up with a big gain or a big loss. However, a well diversified portfolio is more stable as according to statistics, 90% of investment return is derived from asset allocation. This is because a diversified portfolio includes investments across many market segments and sectors that help balance risk and reward.

Think Long Term

The term "long term" may not look very encouraging to you as you have probably witnessed many long term investors losing big money in the financial crisis.

But to think long term doesn't mean you buy a stock sit tight and hope that it will appreciate ten fold or twenty fold in the long run. The basic criterion for a long term investor is that you must be an active investor, active enough to manage your portfolio according to the external environmental changes.

Say for example, in the event of a financial crisis, your portfolio shrank by half, what would you do? A passive investor will feel paralysed and do nothing as he or she is afraid of making more mistakes. This will turn you to a long term loser as you may shun from investing in equities which results in losing a good source of passive income.

With the long term view in mind, an active investor will take the opportunity to lower cost averaging by invest in blue chip stocks during the bear market and sell partially during the bull market.

When you think in terms of states of wealth and not short term profit, you are thinking long term, which is more rational.

Emotionally Independent

An emotionally independent investor does not feel ecstatic or lucky when generating positive returns; nor will the investor feel sad at losing money. If you feel happy with every single gain or sad with each loss, you are probably an emotional investor.

For example, an effective way to be emotionally independent is to overcome the anchoring bias in you. As pointed out earlier, anchoring bias occurs when an investor is influenced by the reference price of a stock. Usually, an investor will purchase a stock when the stock price reaches to a level close to its year low without analysing the fundamental of the stock. Hence, to overcome this emotional bias, you have to set a purchase price yourself according to the fundamental of the stock, and purchase it when it reaches the target level. And do the opposite when you intend to sell a stock. Hence, you focus at the true value of the stock and not your reference point for it.

Research, Research, Research

I always tell people that investment knowledge is the key to success in the world of investment. By reading a lot more than everyone else, you will naturally recognise and welcome opportunities as they show themselves to you. To be a successful investor like Warren Buffett, you must be curious enough to investigate the stock that you are buying. Treat it as investing in a business that you think will generate profits for you in many years to come.

Although some may say that too much information may crowd your mind, but the thought of investing in something that you know of is better than something you don't. Anything else is just speculating.

Money Management

According to Dr. Alexander Elder, the author for "Trading For A Living", the first goal of money management is to ensure survival. The second goal is to earn a steady rate of return.

A novice investor often tries to get rich quickly by investing too much of his or her equity in a single stock and in the process, either by emotion or ignorance, and sometimes a combination of the two, can get wiped out.

Professional traders will make every calculated risk by not risking more than 2% of their equity in one single trade. Although it sounds like a rich man's game but the rationale behind this is to put a solid floor under the amount of damage the market can do to your account.

Take a Time Out

Sometimes during the course of trading, your may encounter rapid heartbeat and shortage of breathe which is due to your adrenaline at work when you feel the risk of trading. This is because you are not sure of the decision that you are about to make and that perhaps you are becoming irrational.

Step away from your desk, go to a quiet place and remind yourself why you are making that particular investment decision. If your explanation sounds rational to you, then you know you are investing properly.

Emotion may hinder your rational thought process and increase your chance of failure. So take your time to digest and analyse thoroughly before acting recklessly.

Don't Obsess Over Daily Fluctuations

It is normal that prices fluctuate every day and it should not change any of your beliefs on where the stock is headed, unless, and only if, the stock undergoes a significant change.

If you are too obsessed over your profits and losses, you'll be investing with a clouded mind. Part of being an unemotional investor is accepting the fact that you will sometimes lose money. As long as you stay active, and think rationally, you will be a winner in the long term.

CHAPTER 17

Margin of Safety

"A margin of safety is achieved when securities are purchased at prices sufficiently below underlying value to allow for human error, bad luck, or extreme volatility in a complex, unpredictable and rapidly changing world."
Seth Klarman

By far the most effective behavioural finance strategy which is highly recommended by many investment gurus is value investing. The virtue of value investing is that investors buy at prices that are already low, there isn't much room for further down play. The following are some strategies employed by three famous investment gurus: Benjamin Graham, Warren Buffett and Seth Klarman.

Benjamin Graham

Benjamin Graham, born in 1894 had witnessed the devastation of the 1929 crash and had since developed resilient techniques that could be used by any investor. He popularized the examination of price-earning (PE) ratios, debt-to-equity ratios, dividend records, net current assets, book values and earnings growth. That earned him the name of the "Father of Value Investing". He brilliantly concocted the 'Margin of Safety' theory that has gained tremendous support across the finance industry. Graham defined margin of safety as the margin at which a stock can be purchased with minimum downside risk.

There are many criteria for Graham's margin of safety investment approach, the most stringent is this: Purchase the stock with price not more than two-thirds of Net Current Asset Value (NCAV).

How to calculate the NCAV?

Net Current Asset Valuation (NCAV) is computed by total current assets less total liabilities.

Example—Calculation for NCAV	
	$'000
Cash at bank	200
Debtors	100
Inventory	100
Total Liabilities	200
# of shares	100
Share price	1.80

In the example, given that the total current assets are $400,000 and total liabilities are $200,000, the net current asset per share is $2 which is lower than the current market price. However, it is still not good enough as according to Graham's criteria, the purchase price must not be more than two-thirds of the NCAV which is $1.33. Therefore, we will not purchase the stock.

The margin of safety for this case is 26% (the difference between current market price and the conservative calculation using Graham's criteria) which is lower than the minimum margin of safety of 33%. Buying at steep discount using the margin of safety approach can help to cushion off the negative surprises in the financial market.

Warren Buffett

While Benjamin Graham has a knack for margin of safety, Warren Buffett's talent is in determining the intrinsic value of a company.

What is intrinsic value?

Every business has an intrinsic value which is defined as the discounted value of the net cash flows that can be taken out of a business during its remaining life. Let's consider a simple illustration.

Example—ABC Ltd

Assuming ABC Ltd has a perpetual life and an estimated free cash flow of $0.20 per share per annum. The current stock price is $3. Next, we need to decide on a discount rate. For this case, we will apply the government bond's return because if we do not invest in ABC Ltd, we could have invested in the government bond. Hence, we'll take the rate of the government bond's rate of 5% as the discount rate.

Intrinsic Value = $\frac{\$0.20}{0.05}$ = $4.

Since the calculated intrinsic value is higher than the current stock price ($4 >$3), ABC Ltd is currently under-valued.

The above illustration is over simplified of course. For the most part, cash flows are is never guaranteed, and the discount rate is arbitrary. That's why the intrinsic value figure is only an approximate value, and not the exact figure. However, the better you understand a business, the better or more accurate is your estimates for the future cash flows and thus more precisely the intrinsic value for the firm.

Warren Buffett made a fortune on Coca-Cola in the 1980s by successfully spotting the intrinsic value of the Coke was much higher than the market price at that time. The market valued Coke at $15.1 billion, while Buffett thought it was worth anywhere from $20.7 billion (based on a 5% growth in its earnings) to $48.3 billion (based on a 15% growth). So, like Benjamin Graham, Buffett felt there was a huge margin of safety on the discount of the intrinsic value and proceeded with the purchase. Now Coca-Cola is the cash cow of Berkshire Hathaway.

Buffett said, "I am a better investor because I'm a businessman; and a better businessman because I'm an investor." And Benjamin Graham famously noted, "Investment is most intelligent when it is most business like."

Seth Klarman

Seth Klarman is the younger version of Warren Buffett. He is a value investor and Portfolio Manager of The Baupost Group, founded in 1983. He published a book in 1991 called "Margin of Safety, Risk Averse Investing Strategies for the Thoughtful Investor", which has since become a value investing classic. The book has long been out of print and the second-hand books were selling on Amazon for $1,200 and eBay for $2,000.

Klarman's Three Investment Principles

Focus on risk

The risk here is not beta. Finance practitioners think that more risk more return. However, Klarman's version of risk is the possibility of suffering a loss; less risk (low chance of losing money) and high margin of safety, the more return. Klarman is careful not to risk his capital and that is why Klarman parked as much as half of his portfolio in cash in 2005 and 2006 until he found investment with enough margin of safety to deploy it. In his shareholder letter, Klarman urges investors to be patient, he said: "Value investors must be over weighted in patience and not to chase over-valued stocks".

Focus on absolute return not relative return

Many fund managers emphasise on relative performance, "the market return was -10%, ours was -3%, we out-perform the market". This is not what Klarman advocates. He thinks that to gain an edge, we should focus on absolute return. Ranking in terms of "not losing money" is more important than whether or not we under-perform or out-perform the market.

Bottom-up approach

Klarman believes that few people can accurately predict the macro economy which makes investment rather difficult if decision is purely based on macro factors which is known as the top-down approach. Unlike top-down approach, bottom-up approach starts with an extensive research on individual stock and company and works out all possible outcomes for that particular stock under different stress test scenarios. This approach can help to identify promising companies that are under-valued in the stock market.

"Value investing by its very nature is contrarian." Klarman believes that value investors are typically wrong initially, since they go against the crowd, and the crowd is the one pushing up the stock prices.

The following is an excerpt from his 2006 letter to his shareholders that I think are some sincere advice for genuine investors:

". . . Growth stocks, at least are interesting; even disciplined value investors are sometimes tempted by the excitement that new technology or rapidly expanding emerging markets seems to promise. Also, many so called value investors are what we call value pretenders, "buy-the-dips" specialists who buy what's down but not necessarily what's cheap. This trading strategy has worked well for a long time, but will disappoint in the next real bear market.

. . . the markets remain inefficient. This is not because of a shortage of timely information, a lack of analytical tools, or inadequate capital. Markets are inefficient because of human nature—innate, deep-rooted, and permanent. People don't consciously choose to invest with emotion—they simply can't help it.

Investors cannot change their stripes and will always exhibit characteristics of greed and fear. They will remain biased towards optimism, interested more in how much they can make rather than how much they might lose. They will be interested in relative, rather than absolute performance. They will want to get rich quick, lured by short term trading strategies, hot IPOs and technical analysis, rather than truly undervalued but long term opportunities. Then, when things go awry, investors will again overreact, selling urgently what has caused them pain without regard for value."

This excerpt says it all! As an equity investor myself, I have to admit that not all my equity investment make positive returns because of the mental biases in me. However I take each mistake as my learning experience towards better investment in future. I believe having the awareness of our mental pitfalls we are able to make more rational investment decisions with longer investment horizons.

CONCLUSION

Though the mental biases described in this book are widely observed, behavioural finance does not claim that all the investors will suffer from the same illusion simultaneously. The susceptibility of an investor to a particular illusion is likely to be affected by many factors such as age, gender, risk preference, investment experience and net worth of the investor.

No matter what, the important lesson is: be a value investor, look for stocks that are deeply discounted, and practice margin of safety. When markets are down, the emotional response for the majority is to react out of fear, and wait until the market is up before getting back in. The successful minority does the opposite, they successfully overcome their fear and proactively takes advantage of the opportunity to buy low.

Before you trade, try the following test to see if you are a rational investor. Have fun!

Mini-Test for Trading Ability
(by Van Tharp, a psychologist)

Answer each question by indicating whether you believe it to be true or false. Think about what typically characterises your behaviour or your belief with respect to the market, and use that as the basis for your answer. Be honest!

1. I sell on bad news.
   T   F

2. I seldom change my mind about a trade once it is made
   T   F

3. Sometimes I buy just to be active in the market.
   T   F

4. I worry about things more than I should.
   T   F

5. My trading rules are written down and review often.
   T   F

6. Business always comes before pleasure for me.
   T   F

7. A falling stock with a price earning ratio of 7 is probably a better long term investment than a rapidly rising stock with a price earning ratio of 27.
   T   F

8. When I get up I eagerly look forward to the day.
   T   F

How did you score?

If you answer any of the questions with the same answer as below, award yourself one point; for question four or eight, score two points for each correct answer.

1. T   2. F 3. T 4. T** 5. F 6. T 7. F 8. F**
Total Score: _____

If you have (score) more than 5 points, then the markets are probably a dangerous place for you as you do not do a lot of homework yourself.

If you have (score) 2-5 points, you are probably better than average, but you still could have difficulty in the markets.

And if you have less than 2 points, then you probably do very well in the markets.

If you want to take other tests by Van Tharp, visit this website: http://tharptradertest.com

ABOUT THE AUTHOR

Pauline Yong is an author and a frequent speaker in Malaysia. She actively promotes financial education for individuals through public and private seminars to educate individuals the basics of stock investing and financial planning. Prior to that, she was an economics lecturer for 15 years.

Pauline holds an MBA in Finance from the University of Leicester (UK), and BBA (Hons) in Finance from York University (Canada). She is also a Certified Financial Technician (CFTe), a Certified Financial Planner (CFP) and a full member of the Society of Technical Analysis (MSTA).